Motion

by Grace Hansen

Abdo
BEGINNING SCIENCE
Kids

Abdo Kids Jumbo is an Imprint of Abdo Kids
abdopublishing.com

abdopublishing.com

Published by Abdo Kids, a division of ABDO, P.O. Box 398166, Minneapolis, Minnesota 55439.
Copyright © 2019 by Abdo Consulting Group, Inc. International copyrights reserved in all countries.
No part of this book may be reproduced in any form without written permission from the publisher.
Abdo Kids Jumbo™ is a trademark and logo of Abdo Kids.

052018

092018

Photo Credits: iStock, Shutterstock

Production Contributors: Teddy Borth, Jennie Forsberg, Grace Hansen

Design Contributors: Dorothy Toth, Laura Mitchell

Library of Congress Control Number: 2017960573

Publisher's Cataloging-in-Publication Data

Names: Hansen, Grace, author.

Title: Motion / by Grace Hansen.

Description: Minneapolis, Minnesota : Abdo Kids, 2019. | Series: Beginning science |
    Includes glossary, index and online resources (page 24).

Identifiers: ISBN 9781532108112 (lib.bdg.) | ISBN 9781532109096 (ebook) |
    ISBN 9781532109584 (Read-to-me ebook)

Subjects: LCSH: Force and energy--Juvenile literature. | Motion--Juvenile literature.

Classification: DDC 531--dc23

Table of Contents

What Is Motion?

When an object changes position it is in motion. There are three main laws of motion. Isaac Newton presented them in 1687.

The First Law

In order for an object's **velocity** to change, a force must act on it. A ball sitting on flat ground will stay there. You apply force when you kick it. The ball's velocity changes.

Friction acts on the ball and slows it down. The air, ground, and net are examples of friction. Without friction the ball would keep moving.

The Second Law

The amount of force needed
to make an object **accelerate**
depends on its **mass**.

The **masses** of a beach ball and a bowling ball are different. It takes much less force to move a beach ball. Force is measured in Newtons (N).

Force needed to accelerate each ball to 1.5 m/s²

Force = mass x acceleration

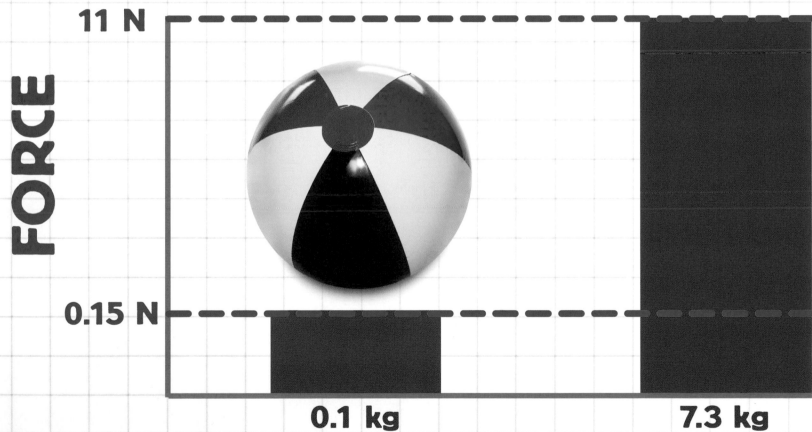

FORCE

11 N

0.15 N

0.1 kg

7.3 kg

MASS

The Third Law

For every action, there is an equal but opposite reaction. You **exert** force on a sled when you pull it. But the sled also pulls on you with the same force.

14

force exerted by dad

force exerted by sled

force on sled
exerted by ground

force on ground
exerted by sled

force on ground
exerted by dad

force on dad
exerted by ground

15

Energy in Motion

When force moves an object, it is called work. Energy is the ability to do work. There are two main types of energy in motion.

Potential energy is energy that could be used to do work. Before dropping in, a skateboarder has potential energy.

Any moving object able to
do work has kinetic energy.
A skateboarder moving down
a ramp has kinetic energy.

Let's Review!

- An object is in motion when it changes position.

- There are three main laws of motion.

- In order for something to move, it needs to be pushed or pulled on. These pushes and pulls are called forces.

- When a force moves an object, it is doing work. In order for work to happen, there must be a source of energy.

Glossary

acceleration – in physics, rate at which velocity changes with time in terms of both speed and direction.

exert – to apply.

friction – the resistance of a surface.

mass – how much matter there is in something. Mass is not the same as weight.

velocity – rate of motion.

Index

Abdo Kids
ONLINE
FREE! ONLINE MULTIMEDIA RESOURCES

Visit **abdokids.com** and use this code to access crafts, games, videos, and more!

Abdo Kids Code:
BMK8112

24